EFFECTIVE LEADERSHIP
FOR ORGANIZATIONS AND OTHER INSTITUTIONS

BY

DR. PHILLIP F. REID

DORRANCE
PUBLISHING CO
EST. 1920
PITTSBURGH, PENNSYLVANIA 15238

Dorrance Publishing Co
585 Alpha Drive
Pittsburgh, PA 15238
Visit our website at *www.dorrancebookstore.com*

ISBN: 978-1-6442-6618-2
eISBN: 978-1-6442-6638-0

Contents

INTRODUCTION

Imagine that all leaders of organizations, schools, and places of worship are long term thinkers who see beyond the day's crisis and know how all the company's or institution's departments affects the other and are current on research-based data. The results would be the creation of a vision for effective leaders that are risk takers, change agents, communicators, that use data to enhance their character, trust, and empower their employees and their organizations. For many effective leaders who are change agents, their leadership began as a phrase that would change lives and human development from the current conditions of that time.

This book identifies characteristics that are common among effective leaders. The book advocates vision, knowledge, effective communication, change agents, collaboration, risk taking, character, use of data, mentorship, legacy, and trustworthiness are emphasized as some of the personal qualities and disposition necessary for effective leadership.

Dr. Martin Luther Kings' "I have a dream" speech of 1962 when he said, "that one day on the red hills of Georgia, the sons of former slaves and sons of former slave owners will be able to sit down together at the table of brotherhood," is an example that a movement for change was given birth when a leader steps out of his comfort zone to take action against what seemed like an impossible mountain to climb (Carson, 1998).

Nelson Mandela's movement, "The international movement of solidarity with the struggle for freedom in South Africa," was one of the largest social movements that made history by the overturn of Apartheid in South Africa. As an effective leader, Nelson Mandela once said, "There is no easy walk to freedom anywhere, and many of us will have to pass through the valley of the shadow of death again and again before we reach the mountain top of our desires" (Mandela, 1990).

President Ronald Reagan's, "Tear down this Wall!" is a line from his speech in West Berlin on June 12th, 1987 that called for the leader of the Soviet Union, Mikhail Gorbachev, to break down the barrier that was erected in 1961 which had divided West and East Berlin.

President Reagan once said, "We welcome change and openness for America believes that freedom and security go together, that the advance of human liberty can only strengthen the course of world peace" (Walsh, 1997).

The wall was later torn down in 1989 and resulted in a unified Germany.

Tarana Burke who had coined the "Me Too" phrase in 2006 to encourage every woman who had survived sexual harassment or assault to come forward with their story. Ms. Burke wanted to help African-American women and girls who had also survived sexual violence. A decade later, the Me Too movement is amplified by women of color and Caucasians. As an activist, Me Too grew out of Tarana Burke's work with young girls in poor communities. Burke recalled that, "People would call her trouble," Burke said, "and she was trouble because she was a survivor" (Wellington, 2018).

In 2017, the Me Too movement has brought to light many abuses by men in organizations in the movie industry, broad casting, places of worship, and educational institutions to name a few.

In 2018, the survivors of the Parkland High School shooting began the Never Again movement. David Hogg is one of the students of Marjory Stoneman Douglass High School in Parkland, Florida who started the Never Again movement. The students advocate for stricter gun control after the mass shooting at their school and have confronted the politicians and the National Rifle Association head-on just four days after the school shooting.

In less than a month, law makers passed a resolution that was signed into law by the governor of Florida to increase the age to buy any firearm from 18 years to 21 years and made illegal bump stocks that converts rifles into an automatic weapon. (Sanchez, 2018)

In this era of mistrust in leaders, now, more than ever, there is the need for leaders with integrity that can develop the characteristics of trustworthiness.

Effective leaders must earn the trust of employee, congregants, and students by maintaining their personal character that is founded on strong moral values.

Dr. Myles Munroe said that, "Trust is not a gift or a talent but a product of time-tested character forged in the midst of life's trials" p. 82 (Munroe, The Principles and Power of Vision. Keys to achieving Personal and Corporate Destiny, 2003).

Leaders are in highly visible positions that make them targets that are vulnerable to temptation. He/she therefore must set for him or herself high standards that he/she maintains regardless of the situation that is presented. Effective leaders know that to be trusted by followers is a process that occurs over time. Effective leaders maintain their integrity and character to ensure that trust is protected.

Webster 1995 defines the noun effect as "a result or product of some cause or agency or a consequence. To bring about, produce as a result, achieve or accomplish. The adjective effective adapted to produce an effect or efficient" (Webster, 1995 International Edition).

My Dad's Community Leadership

"Vision is the primary motivator of human action, and therefore, everything we do should be because of the vision God has placed in our hearts" p 32. (Munroe, The Principles and Power of Vision. Keys to achieving Personal and Corporate Destiny, 2003).

My dad, a young missionary in the semi-urban parish of St. Catherine on the island of Jamaica, was sent to a rural community in St. Elizabeth to establish a wing of the Pentecostal Church. In his new community, the farmers cultivated long term crops and spent three to six months of the year away in North America, picking apples in the northern state of New York and harvesting sugar cane in the southern state of Florida.

My dad needed to provide for his family on a continuous basis. He introduced the production of short-term cash crops to supplement his stipend from his ministerial work. His visionary leadership enabled him to lease land spaces for his cash crops until he could make a down payment on a five-acre property, where he eventually built a two-bedroom home. He employed young men from the community and taught them the husbandry of short-term cash crops.

Today, more than 50 years later, the community has small farmers with more than 90% of their crops as short-term cash crops. The parish of St. Elizabeth in

Jamaica West Indies is known widely as the Breadbasket of the island because of the many short-term cash crops that can be grown throughout the year.

At that time, I did not see my dad as a visionary leader. My father used his vision as a value to guide his living.

CHAPTER 1

Who is an effective leader?

An effective leader is one who is creative and has the ability to produce profits or increase in quantity, quality, tangible results that are of value in wealth, industrial artistic, or literary contributions in the society or the ability to positively affect the people they lead. Webster, 1995, describes the noun "leader" as "one who leads, conduct; guides or command." The noun leadership is "the office or position of a leader."

What is effective leadership?

Effective leadership is the ability of an individual to lead a company, organization, or group and successfully influence the group, company, or organization to efficiently produce above and beyond its normal expected outcome or accomplishment. Effective leaders are committed to a lifelong level of proficiency that is centered on achieving a personal vision. (Green, 2013)

Webster 1995 describes vision as, "a mental representation of external object; a fantasy; inspired revelation; foresight; the ability to anticipate and make provision for future events" (Webster, 1995 International Edition).

What is leadership?

Leadership is the capacity to influence others through inspiration generated by a passion motivated by a vision birth by conviction produced by a purpose

(Munroe, The Power of Character in Leadership. How Values, Morals, Ethics, and Principles Affect Leadership, 2014).

Purpose is self-discovery that you were born with a gift that is important to the world. Your vision is like a seed seeing itself as a tree with fruits. In some cultures, some citizens are made to feel that they are not important, which lead to their inability to achieve their purpose. In cultures where everyone is motivated to be an important individual, they are more inclined to become successful because they believe in the conviction to realize their vision. Promoting leadership potential into every individual will result in you always getting what you need.

Followers are attracted to effective leaders because of their passion and dedication to their vision to improve people, self, organizations, and institutions of worship (Munroe, The Power of Character in Leadership. How Values, Morals, Ethics, and Principles Affect Leadership, 2014).

Why do we need leadership?

"Leadership exists for the purpose of guiding others to a better future, enabling them to develop in greater way: to improve themselves" (Munroe, Work Book. Discovering The Leader you were Meant to be! Becoming a Leader, 2009).

Effective leaders use the power of inspiration to motivate people to align themselves in fulfilling the vision of an organization. Effective leaders invest time and resources and their expertise into followers, thereby empowering them to become leaders. The ultimate goal of effective leadership is to produce leaders from those who were once followers. The inspiration of effective leaders will stimulate followers to strive to change their own priorities to become the best that they can be as they work towards their own visions and fulfillment in leadership positions.

Effective leaders empower others by encouraging teamwork and showing appreciation for creativity in others. When collaboration and creativity is encouraged in followers, they in turn impart their abilities and talents towards fulfilling the vision of the organization. This can only be achieved when the effective leader establishes an environment that fosters mutual respect and maintains a cohesive team of employees where each unique strength enhances the productivity of the organization.

Effective leaders are good managers of their personal resources. He/she plans for the involvement of the people and material resources to achieve the vision of the organization both for short-term and for future endeavors. Effective leaders monitor progress and make adjustments to their vision plans to promote continuous improvement in the organization. By monitoring progress, effective leaders can revise their plans as they develop assessment and accountability systems to monitor and sustain the organizations progress.

Leadership and Organizations

An organization can be defined as "the rational coordination of activities of a number of people for the achievement of some common goal, through division of labor and functions, through a hierarchy of authority and responsibility" p. 9. (Schein, 1992). An organization is an open social system that receives resources (input) from external environment, transforms that input through an internal system, and returns it to the external environment (output) (Katz & Kahn, 1978). Scott defined an organization as a social structure that is created by individuals to support the collaborative pursuit of specified goals (Scott W. , 2003).

The effective leader knows how to ensure that the parts of the organization that are interdependent and interrelated are developed to maintain an operational environment that is efficient, safe and effective in promoting the success for all within the organization.

Effective leaders unite those they lead

Abraham Lincoln once stated that,

"A house divided against itself cannot stand. I believe this government cannot endure permanently half slave and half free…. I do not expect the house to fall, but I do expect it will cease to be divided. It will become all one thing or all the other" p. 112. (Savory, 2010).

Abraham Lincoln in the 1858 Illinois Republican Convention in his bid to become Senator, as an effective leader, he boldly spoke out against slavery. As an effective leader, he was willing to put his career on the line, and eventually his life, for what he believed was right for the United States of America.

"Lincoln had never been a man who placed his own political ambitions ahead of what he felt was right" p. 168. (Savory, 2010).

Abraham Lincoln went on to become the President of the United States. Historians state that President Lincoln had done more to end slavery in the United States than anyone before or after him. In his relentless fight against the enslavement of African-Americans, President Lincoln made many enemies, especially the southerners who were slave owners who depended on slaves to work on their plantations. President Abraham Lincoln was eventually assassinated, and at his funeral, the words of hope and encouragement of one of his closing speeches was recorded.

"I leave you, hoping that the lamp of liberty will burn in your bosoms until there shall no longer be a doubt that all men are created free and equal" p. 185 (Savory, 2010).

Perhaps no other president of the United States, past or future, has so exemplified the view that all men are created equal. President Lincoln believed and lived by that principle. His extraordinary leadership skills enabled him to free thousands of African-Americans from slavery.

CHAPTER 2

Who is an effective visionary leader?

"Show me a leader without a vision, and I'll show you someone who isn't going anywhere. At best, he/she is traveling in circles" (Maxwell, The 21 Irrefutable Laws of Leadership. Follow Them and People Will Follow You, 1998).

Vision comes from within and is drawn from natural gifts or talents. Effective leaders are visionary who see beyond the norm.

An effective leader is a visionary leader who can see into the future. He sees what may seem impracticable under present circumstances. The Wright brothers, Wilbur and Orville, on December 17th, 1903, Orville made the first powered flight at 120 feet; Wilbur, in the fourth and longest, made 825 feet in 59 seconds. After many failed experimental attempts to make a glider that could carry a person, their experiment marked the turning point in attempts by man to fly. The Wright brothers are examples of effective leaders that used their failures as an inspiration to achieve their vision to fly. In 1903, the Wright's compiled tables and figures from which one might design an airplane that could lift itself and fly. (Kelly, 1994)

In less than a century, the aerospace industry has grown into the largest and most technically complex manufacturing industry in the United States. Boeing, one of the largest companies in the area of aerospace, had sales of nearly $3 billion in 2015 with profits forecasted between 96 to 98 billion U.S. dollars in 2018. The vision for man to fly may have been a fantasy or imaginary dream for the Wright brothers in 1901, but in 2018, it is still one of the largest industries that make billions of dollars in profits.

Effective leaders in organizations outside and inside the field of education advocate vision and effective communication as traits that empower followers. Sam Walton, founder of Walmart, had a passion and vision to provide consumers with low cost products and a wide variety under one roof. He was an effective communicator that empowered investors to share his vision. In 2018, Walmart super stores are located in almost every state in the U.S. and is a place where shoppers can go to get just about any type of product that they need for use in and outside their home.

Seeing beyond what can be seen.

Dr. Myles Munroe (2015), in a presentation, described a story of a little girl on her father's shoulder and that of a visionary leader. "The family was on the upper deck of a cruise ship talking about the beautiful scenery. The young girl that was short in stature could hardly see over the deck of the ship. Eventually, she convinced her dad, who lifted her and seated her on his shoulder. The young girl in amazement said, 'Dad, I can see further than my eyes can see'" (Munroe, The Principles and Power of Vision. Keys to achieving Personal and Corporate Destiny, 2003).

Effective leaders are visionaries who have a vision for the future that cannot be seen with the naked eyes.

Communicating the Vision

Effective leaders engage stake holders in fulfilling the organization's vision and mission by asking key stakeholders to assess the effectiveness of the current vision and mission regularly. During the organization improvement process, engaging stakeholders with periodic sessions to assess the effectiveness of the current vision and mission is one of its most authentic activities.

An effective leader is most likely to establish effective communication with stakeholders if information is presented to them in a timely manner in a variety of digital and printed format. The best initial actions for effective leaders to take when building a partnership with community groups is to develop a shared vision to support the success of the organization.

When stakeholders are committed to the success of an organization in achieving its goal, effective leaders must include stakeholders in developing or updating the organizations vision regularly because they have the investment capacity to promote the positive outcomes set forth in the vision.

Munroe noted that it is a deeply distressing fact that we all have been given unique visions, but too many of us bury our dreams in lesser existence, making ourselves a grave yards of God's precious treasure (Munroe, The Principles and Power of Vision. Keys to achieving Personal and Corporate Destiny, 2003). We settle for little things in life, such as getting a good education in order to get a good job and get a nice home, instead of risk pursuing our entrepreneurial dreams and inventions.

CHAPTER 3

Risk and effective leadership

"Failure is often far less painful and debilitating than the fear of failure. If you take away a person's right to fail, you take away his/her right to succeed" p. 215 (Fullan M., 2007).

Effective Leaders are risk takers and see a failure as a learning experience.

Fascinated by the promise of the internal combustion engine and its application to a self-propelled vehicle, Henry Ford constructed a one-cylinder gasoline motor in 1893 (Johnson, 1994).

He went on to build his first car that was a light carriage powered by a two-cylinder engine in June 1896. Henry Ford's company, the "Detroit Automobile Company." was forced into bankruptcy in less than two years.

A group of investors and Mr. Ford organized to form the Ford Motor Company in 1903. Free to follow his own ideas as majority stock holder in the company, Ford found overwhelming success from sales of the low-priced Model N. Ford, then moved to the Model T. In its first year, more than 10,000 Model T's were sold. By the end of its production in 1927, 15 million Model T's had changed American motoring lifestyle.

Ford's growth was propelled by his learning in failure. His failed experience that led to the bankruptcy of the Detroit Automobile Company became a learning experience that enabled him to reflect and make sense of the failure.

Effective leaders use risk taking and learning from pass failures to ask themselves reflective questions that occurred as a result of their failure.

9

a.   What caused the failure to occur?

b.   What did I learn from the experience?

c.   If I had to do it over again, what would I do differently?

d.   How or where do I get help?

Why take the risk?

Fullan noted that to lead others towards profound levels of learning is to risk; to promote personal and organizational renewal is to risk (Fullan M. , 2007).

To create organizations, learning institutions, houses of worship, and industries hospitable to human learning is to risk.

In Aesop's fables, a number of mice colony called a meeting to decide how to best rid themselves of a cat that had killed their friends. They collaborated on many plans that were rejected. Finally, a young mouse suggested that a bell should be hung around the cat's neck, that they might, in future, have a warning to enhance escape from the incumbent danger from the cat. The suggestion was received with overwhelming support by more than 90% of the mice. However, an old mouse who had been silent for some time got up and said, "While I consider the plan to be very smart and could prove successful if it were possible, I would like to know who is going to take the risk to bell the cat?"

"The trouble is if you don't risk anything, you risk everything" (Jung, 1962).

Effective leaders who are not afraid to risk evolve into change agents.

Having read different books on leadership, I have found that effective leaders don't play by manmade rules. They make their own rules and are game changers who are not afraid to take risks that propel them to be creative in changing how the world communicates and consumers use their products.

Embracing Risk

"No matter how great the talent or effort, some things just take time" (Ilian, 2016).

One may ask, what is one of the attributes that sets an effective leader apart from other leaders? It is his or her willingness to take risks. Effective leaders see adversity as an opportunity to face the many challenges and use the experience as a spring to propel them forward towards achieving their vision. Risk creates the drive and determination to make your organization, and if possible, the world a better place for humanity.

Warren Buffett is an effective leader in his field and has faced many challenges, but he never backs down when faced with roadblocks. He believes that as an investor, you embrace the short-term loss and the idea of long-term growth.

In 1997, Amazon's stock was trading at $20 a share and most investors sold their stock while Warren Buffett bought the stocks that investors considered was a foolish investment. In 2016, Amazon's stock was trading at $310 per share. Currently in 2018, Amazon's stock is trading at close to $400 a share. As an effective leader, Warren Buffet was willing to take the risk of buying the stocks at $20 a share because he saw opportunity for changes and long-term growth.

CHAPTER 4

The Process of Change

"One aspect of effective leadership is the ability to manage change while keeping the organization moving towards goals over time" (Hawkins, 2011).

Effective leaders are change agents that ensures that the members of the organization buys in and support the proposed changes by developing a clear action plan to meet the successful outcome that is in line with the organization's vision.

What is change?

Smith defined change as any intentional shift in the way the organization does business as that organization relates to the strategic position of other competing organizations (Smith, 2002).

Change is a process rather than a single event that takes place with the organization, group, products, or person. Effective leaders are aware that organizations that are flexible react appropriately to changes in environmental conditions are more successful in this era of new technology, culture, or continuous improvement in curriculum and individual development.

A principal, faced with impending restructuring, perceptively described his conflicting feeling about change:

"I feel like a bird that has been caged by rules and regulations for a long time. With school reform, the door is now open. I'm standing at the edge. Will I dare to fly out? I am beginning to realize that the bars of the cage that have imprisoned me all these years have been the very same bars that have protected me from the hawks and falcons out there. I'm not sure I'm going to fly?" p. 217, 218 (Fullan M. , 2007).

Do you fear change?

Effective leaders use change as a motivational vehicle to inspire important ideas that influence the development of the organizations infrastructure. Greater success is awaiting you outside the bars that you thought was your safety net.

In T. D. Jakes 2014, Instinct, he noted that in the instinct to jump,

"Some are pushed, but some fear the low-grade life of playing it safe and jump into a waiting destiny they sense deep within. Curiously enough, this type of persons become the people we end up reading about, watching on television, listening to on our iPods, and following on Twitter. They are what I call Jumpers – people willing to jump out of their nests or cage and into the free fall of the jungle, where they must survive by their instinct" p. 87. (Jakes, Instinct. The Power to Unleash Your Inborn Drive, 2014).

Steve Jobs, the visionary founder of Apple, declared the most recognizable brand in the world, surpassing Coca-Cola for the first time in sales of the product.

Jobs, who co-founded Apple in 1976, had to sell Wozniak's Apple I personal computer. The duo gained fame and wealth a year later for the Apple II, one of the first highly successful mass-produced personal computers. Following a long power struggle, Jobs was forced out of Apple in 1985. (Foremenski, 2016) Because of Jobs' ability to adjust to the process of change, he needed to modify his adaptation to maintain flexibility and react appropriately to new environmental conditions to survive.

After leaving Apple, Jobs found NEXT, a computer platform development company specializing in advanced state-of-the-art computer technology for higher-education and business markets.

Adapting to Change

Change is based on building a new organization and gradually transferring people from the old to the new structure (Nikols, 2003).

In one strategy for change in environmental-adaptability is the assumption that people oppose loss and disruption but can adapt. Steve Jobs was forced to leave Apple, but the change enabled him to build a new organization and work on new products that would gradually transfer people from the old way of using computers.

In 1997, Apple acquired and merged NEXT, allowing Jobs to become the CEO once again, reviving the company at the verge of bankruptcy (Foremenski, 2016). In the "think different" advertising campaign, Jobs developed a line of products that would have larger cultural ramification. The products, iMac, iTunes, Apple Store, iPad, iPhone, App Store, are all based on Jobs' Next step platform.

Pushing Steve Jobs from the security of the cage at Apple, the company he co-founded required that he disengage some behaviors that he developed within his last environment and develop instincts of change that would enable him to survive in the wild.

As a child in the 1970's, I can remember my dad carrying his small transistor radio around with him everywhere he went. By the 1980's, every young man's desire was to have a 10 to 20 pound boom box radio on his shoulder and his cassette tapes with the latest hit songs. Change is the process that led to the introduction of the cell phone that in 2000 was small enough to carry everywhere with you and it was equipped with the internet, TV, and with the apps for any music you wanted at your fingertips by 2018.

CHAPTER 5

Communication and using data in Leadership

An effective leader can use communication to identify problems and apply the appropriate remedy to the problem in its early stage. Bolman and Deal noted that crisis is an acid test to leadership because in the heat of the moment leaders sometimes hesitate until events pass them by (Bolman & Deal, 2013). However, effective leaders prepare resources in advance to address the needs that the crisis may present.

Super Storm Sandy emerged out of the Atlantic Ocean approximately a week before the presidential election of Mitt Romney and President Barack Obama in 2012. The storm was a major threat to the east coast of the United States and a challenge to both candidates. Mitt Romney had favored defunding FEMA, the Federal Emergency Management Association in a previous debate. On the other hand, President Barack Obama increased FEMA's resources and made the decision to mobilize the resources to the east coast in anticipation to Sandy's natural disaster.

President Obama could have stumbled as his predecessor, President George W. Bush, had done during hurricane Katrina in 2005 by declaring that all was well when some citizens were still trapped by flood water in their homes. Just before Sandy hit, President Obama, who was campaigning in Florida, cut short his campaign and went back to Washington. When he got back to Washington, he ordered relief to the forecasted affected areas, communicated with governors and mayors throughout the east coast of the

United States, and travelled to scenes of destruction to offer comfort and reassurance.

As an effective leader, he put the needs of the country first and implemented a state of emergency along the entire east coast. He could have continued to campaign for his re-election, but he identified the storm as a problem that would disrupt the lives of the American people and chose to address the problem by mobilizing FEMA resources in the anticipated storm damaged areas.

President Obama's ability to provide the resources for the east coast made the intended problem caused by Hurricane Sandy less of a problem because he communicated with his team and mobilized most, if not all, of the resources that were needed to bring stability to the states along the east coast that were affected by Hurricane Sandy.

Communication and Leadership

Effective leaders who are change agents use communication or consultation to collaborate with all stake holders. "Communication is the lifeblood of organizations, learning institutions, and places of worship because it is a process that links the individual, the group, and the organization" p. 176. (Lunenburg & Ornstein, 1996).

When there is the presence of effective communication, relationships are built, trust is established, and respect is gained (Green, 2013). (Green, 2013) Studies in the field of education and other organization consistently report that most effective leaders of the change process convey a "contagious" or "infectious" passion, energy, and conviction about the ability of the staff to accomplish great things collectively (Fullan M. G., 2002) (Goleman, 2006) (Kanter, 1982) (Marzano, Waters, & McNulty, School leadership that works: From research to results, 2005) (Dufour, Dufour, & Eake, 2008). President Ronald Reagan knew that the interpersonal collaboration and sharing of information was necessary to bring about the positive change in the country at that time when double digit unemployment was the order of the day. President Reagan would sit at the gathering of close advisors as an interested participant rather than as the leader who orders the discussion (Walsh, 1997). As an effective leader, President Regan organized collaborative teams that used their collective experiences to accomplish shared goals in making his term as president successful.

Communication and Sharing of Information

Studies have shown that higher levels of communication, teamwork, and responsiveness to analysis of data are associated with better output in organizations.

Guarino in a 1974 study noted that, "In the area of leadership, there is no talent more essential than one's ability to communicate" (Guarino, 1974). Effective leaders use communication to link individuals and teams within the organization. Green concluded that through effective communications, relationships are built, trust is established, and respect is gained (Green, 2013). Effective leaders use communication to enhance the productivity of the organization towards its vision. Communication is the vehicle used by effective leaders to transmit messages to advocate, nurture, and delegate responsibility to enable followers in the development of their potential and professional growth. Effective leaders use communication as a vehicle to transmit messages and also to receive input from members of the organization.

Consequently, Green believes that the leader's ability to communicate with others is tantamount to the organization operating in an efficient and effective manner (Green, 2013). Effective communication creates a mutual sharing of ideas through a variety of communication skills to ensure that the receiver gives meaning to the message based on their knowledge and experience.

Effective leaders that are effective communicators are active listeners that are approachable and are attentive to both the content of the message and the disposition of the listener. Green acknowledged that feedback given to the sender must be clear, that the message was appreciated both in meaning and feelings with which the message was conveyed (Green, 2013).

Effective use of Data in Leadership

"One of the major purposes of data-based decision-making is to make school improvement that have the most significant impact on the students being served" (Hawkins, 2011).

Effective leaders who are change agents are always using data to improve themselves, learning institutions, places of worship, and organizations. In the school system, it is often said that data drives instruction. In business or organization, data is used to drive productivity. Schools and organization that do not properly analyze data are less likely to be successful. President Clinton, as an effective leader, used data to ensure the effective and efficient use of funding to garner his success as a president.

In his 1999 State of the Union speech, President Clinton told the nation,

"Because of the hard work and high purpose of the American people, these are good times for America. We have more than 14 million new jobs, the lowest unemployment in 24 years, the lowest core inflation in 30 years, incomes are rising, and we have the highest home ownership in history. Crime has dropped for a record five years in a row…. Ladies and gentlemen, the state of the union is strong" p. 7-8. (Schuman, 1999).

In the previous years prior to President Clinton's presidency, unemployment was on the rise, inflation was on the increase, and crime across the country was at its highest level. President Clinton used many data gathering tools within the public and private sector to create the change in the direction of the country.

President Clinton was and is criticized about some of the uneasiness and statements he used to address the state of crime in minority communities. What made the difference in the United States successful achievements that was echoed in President Clinton's 1999 State of the Union speech was that as an effective leader, the President effectively gathered data and then performed the preliminary diagnosis of the information in order to reduce crime across the nation.

Data Assessment and Analysis

"What matters is that you vigorously assemble evidence/data-quantifications and qualitations to track your progress" p.7. (Collins, Good to great and the social sectors. Why business thinking is not the answer, 2005).

Effective school leaders prepare their school improvement plan by looking at survey and assessment data to use for identifying the academic needs of students. Their goal is to analyze performance data by grade level and subject and also by the results of parent questionnaires on school programs. By examining both quantitative and qualitative data, the effective leader can use summative test scores and formative teacher assessments to provide measurable data about student performance. The parent surveys when disaggregated can identify perceptions or beliefs that may be inhibiting the success of the schools efforts to meet the educational needs of the students. By examining both quantitative and qualitative data, an effective district/school leader can form the most complete picture of the educational needs of students.

In a time of reduced funding and the need to improve the infrastructure of an organization, effective leaders can best help ensure that sufficient resources are available to achieve the company's vision and goals by using performance data to identify areas of greatest weakness and making those areas a priority in terms of resource allocation and technological development.

Data and Feedback

"Effective administrators must strive to collect evidence/data from different sources, using varied methods, and do so for a sufficient time period to ensure that what was observed represents the reality of what actually occurred" p. 937. (Hawkins, 2011).

Effective leaders gather data and share their findings with their clients or teams within the organization. These leaders meet in person with target groups to share what was learned and to discuss next steps collaboratively. The data is more convincing when the results is analyzed by a team of experts/people and respondents are readily available to clarify doubts that may arise in the results. Effective leaders use these strategies to persuade doubters to buy-in to a new concept that will ensure the success of the organization.

Diagnosis of the problem

"Feedback should be corrective, timely, and specific to a criterion" (Marzano, Pickering, & Pollock, Classroom instruction that works, 2001).

Effective leaders come together with all stakeholders to do diagnosis of the problem to ensure that the diagnosis and recommendation is understood and accepted through the ongoing collaborative process by which the data and diagnosis are shared with the relevant group leaders and individuals. They must rely on supportable researched data to dictate that appropriate answers addresses the problem.

The rapid uptick in crime during the late 1980's in the United States and leading into the 1990's became one concern that many Americans desired to see decline. The nation's urban cities were marred by crime and violence perpetuated by armed gangs. President Clinton discussed his new crime bill and said that he hoped this would give our young people the chance to walk to school and home in safety and to be in school in safety instead of dodging bullets.

President Clinton in his 1994 State of the Union address in the most compelling moment in his speech came when he said, "Let's be honest. Our problems go way beyond the scope of government. They're rooted in the loss of values and the disappearance of work and the breakdown of our families and communities. My fellow Americans, we can cut deficit, create jobs … and pass the toughest crime bill in history…. The American people have got to want to change from within if we're going to bring back work and family and community" p. 88 (Kent, 1994).

President Clinton knew from the data that if there were new programs in place in the urban cities for empowering the youth through employment, there would be more investment in those areas that needed it the most. The end result was the reduction in crime and the increase funding expenditure for fighting crime in the urban cities.

As an effective leader, President Clinton used diagnosis of the crime problem with emphasis on data collection to present a crime bill that provided the funding for more police officers for the inner cities, stricter gun laws, and the "three strikes and you are out" rule.

Crime, if left unchecked, can lead to investor reluctance to invest in the country. If there are no investors or organizations where the citizens can be gainfully employed, there will be increased unemployment in the inner cities. The increased unemployment can lead to the ideal conditions that can result in a sharp rise in violent crime. President Clinton and his administration took a stance to stop rising crime in the country. His decision led to historic reduction of crime across the country from the 1990's and into the year 2000 and beyond.

Planning for Action

Failing to plan is planning to fail.

"Bill Gates' individual achievements have been some of the most remarkable of the last century. No entrepreneurs before Gates had ever been as successful in the sheer speed with which his business empire was built" p. 100 (Ilian, 2016).

Bill Gates' effective leadership in planning and dedication to marketing and public relations resulted in him spending many hours travelling and participating in interviews in order to present Microsoft products to potential consumers. The successful launch of Windows 95 gained for him billions of dollars in revenue for Microsoft in an era where branding and public relations were the order of the day. Ilian stated that, "How much of Microsoft success was due to its accompanying marketing campaign is hard to quantify, however, it is certainly reasonable to suppose that it had a significant effect in making

Microsoft Windows 95 perhaps the single most popular operating system ever" p. 88. (Ilian, 2016).

Bill Gates used his public relations skills to effectively change how the world communicates. We can all learn valuable lessons from Gates' experiences in adaptability and branding that made him the world's richest man 12 years in a row.

CHAPTER 6

Leading the fight for what is right

"No self-respecting freedom fighter will take orders from the government on how to wage the freedom struggle against the same government and who his allies in the freedom struggle should be. To obey such instructions would be a violation of the long-standing and fruitful solidarity which distinguishes our liberation movement and a betrayal of those who worked so closely and suffered so much with us for almost 70 years" (Mandela, 1990).

Data showed that for more than 70 years, the black South Africans were treated inhumanely by the white South Africans. As an effective leader, Nelson Mandela put all on the line to fight for what he believed was a true cause. Prior to 1990, the people of South Africa who were not Caucasian or white struggled to release themselves from the oppression of Apartheid.

Apartheid is a philosophy of white supremacy. It promoted the separation of races and extended white social privilege and political dominance.

This led to the implementation of segregation where black South Africans were relocated in to concentrated regions of the country while the white population occupied fertile land spaces. Segregation resulted in unequal education and suppressive job discrimination. The restriction of black South Africans ownership of land and property was in order at that time during Apartheid. The Apartheid laws authorized the creation of African reservations and ultimately restricted black South African ownership of land and property to only 13% of the country.

The African National Congress

As early as 1948, Mandela dedicated his life to fight against Apartheid unjust laws. Mandela and his friends believed that they could force the white to change unfair treatment of black South Africans. Mandela became leader of the African National Congress (ANC) and launched the defiance against unjust law campaign where volunteers across the country were encouraged to do boycotts and strikes. After the Sharpeville massacre of 1960, where 69 unarmed child protestors were killed, Mandela was willing to put his life on the line to organize a national strike and day of mourning.

Mandel was first arrested and spent five months in prison. Upon his release, he travelled the continent of Africa and went to Europe to raise support for the ANC. Mandela was again arrested upon his return to South Africa and sentenced to life imprisonment in 1964. As an effective leader, President Mandela fought for what he knew was right and was willing to die for that cause.

At his trial, Nelson Mandela said, "I have dedicated myself to this struggle for the African people.... I cherished the ideal of a democratic and free society … it is an ideal for which I am prepared to die" p. 45 (Kramer, 2008).

Mandela spent 27 years in prison. At age 75 in 1994, Nelson Mandela became the first black South African President. President Mandela's belief in a just cause eventually lead to the abolishment of Apartheid, the freedom of black South Africans to vote, travel, become land owners, and have access to better educational opportunities.

Taking a stand for what is right.

Rosa Parks stood up for what is right when she bravely sat in the front of the bus instead of moving to a seat in the back of the bus. Parks' defiance to not give up her seat to a white passenger eventually lead to her arrest and to the Montgomery Bus Boycott. Ms. Rosa Parks lost her job as a seamstress but was effective in sparking the resistance to racial segregation, which led to collaboration of civil rights leaders, including Dr. Martin Luther King Jr.

Dr. Martin Luther King gained national and international prominence in the civil rights movement as an effective leader who believed in non-violence. In his last speech, he echoed that he was not afraid to die for what he knew was right and that the central truth of the American experience was that we were all created equal. He stated in a speech that:

"Like anybody, I would like to live a long life. Longevity has its place. But I'm not concerned about that now. I just want to do God's will. He's allowed me to go up to the mountain. I've looked over … I've seen the Promised Land. I may not get there with you …But we as a people will get to the Promised Land…. I'm not worried about anything. I'm not fearing any man" p.138 (Carson, 1998).

Dr. Martin Luther King recalled in his autobiography that his angriest moment in his life was when he and his teacher, Mrs. Bradley, were ordered by a white driver to give up their seats to white passengers that boarded the bus that they were on in-route to Atlanta. The driver began cursing at them because they didn't move quickly enough to suit him. They had to ride for 90 miles to Atlanta, standing in the isle of the bus. He grew up with segregation and the barbarous acts as the Ku Klux Klan used violent methods of hanging, beating, and shooting African-Americans to preserve segregation and to keep the negro in his place.

A turning point occurred in his life one summer during his late teens when he observed the oppressive conditions and injustice of the negro and poor white Americans who were working in a plant that employed both negroes and whites. In the preceding summer, just before college, he had the opportunity to work on a tobacco plantation in Stanberry, Connecticut and was surprised to see black people eating in restaurants of their choice. He noted:

"I had never thought that a person of my race could eat anywhere, but we ate in one of the finest restaurants in Hartford" p. 10 (Carson, 1998).

On his trip back from the northern states to the southern states, it became difficult to understand why he could ride anywhere on the train from New York to Washington, but from Washington to Atlanta, he had to sit behind a curtain in one of the dining cars.

Making adjustments as an Effective Leader

Dr. Martin Luther King could never adjust or feel comfortable with separate waiting rooms and separate restrooms because he believed that separate was always the same as unequal. Dr. King became fascinated with the essays of Henry David Thoreau. That was his first contact with the theory of nonviolent resistance. The theory came alive in the civil rights movement.

As an effective leader in the civil rights movement, his theory of nonviolence resonated in the freedom rides, peaceful protests in Alabama, Georgia, and the bus boycott in Montgomery as he demonstrated to make racial justice a reality. His fascination by Gandhi's campaigns of nonviolent resistance further inspired him to a life of nonviolent resistance. Dr. Martin Luther King's effective leadership enabled the change in the civil rights movement where many privileges, such as equal education for African-American children and the right for adults to vote, were not the order of the day for African-Americans.

CHAPTER 7

Character Protects Leadership

"Character is the most powerful force a leader can cultivate because it protects leadership. It will enable you to be a success, personally and professionally, as you carry out your purpose, vision, and goals in life" (Munroe, The Principles and Power of Vision. Keys to achieving Personal and Corporate Destiny, 2003).

If character is the most powerful force a leader can cultivate, we must ask, "Why is character necessary for effective leadership?"

Webster defines character as the combination of qualities distinguishing any person or class of person with moral force or of good reputation. What makes moral force and the need for a good reputation important?

Character is similar to that of someone working many years to invest in the purchase of a house. One night, the gentle breeze from an open window caused the flames from a lit candle to ignite with the curtains or drapes on the window. Within minutes, this home that took years to become a reality is destroyed by fire in a few minutes. The key to rising and not falling is sound character. Character is measured by the belief in what is moral and just.

Developing values and codes of ethics protects leaders from the negative effects of other influences.

"Good character or moral force is like a personal security system for your life" (Munroe, The Power of Character in Leadership. How Values, Morals, Ethics, and Principles Affect Leadership, 2014).

It takes many years for aspiring leaders to be successful. However, what took years to build is destroyed in a day. Once you lose the trust of colleagues, it's very hard to regain.

"The German electronics giant Siemens approached the question, "Should we pay someone a bribe if that will help us bring in business?" Like many German firms, Siemens at that time routinely paid bribes in foreign countries whenever that seemed to be the local custom. When German law changed in 1999, Siemens changed, too, "… by funding creative ways to hide bribes" p. 393 (Bolman & Deal, 2013). Eventually, several top company personnel went to jail (Schubert & Miller, 2008). However, the greatest cost for Siemens' was the undermining of the company's image that customers could trust to obey laws and act with sound character. The company had to spend some 2.6 billion dollars in fines.

The Culture of Trust in Leadership

"Trust is the cornerstone of the leader-follower relationship, where followers feel confident that the leader speaks truthfully, keeps confidences and respect all members of the organization" (Sousa, 2003).

Consequently, the mutual respect between leaders and followers is a factor that enables all members to contribute to the success of the organization. In order to foster positive interpersonal relationships and open lines of communication, effective leaders must build a culture of trust within their organization.

Ciancutti and Steding propose that in a culture of trust, effective leaders are consistent in words, actions, deeds, and there are no gaps between what the leader says or does (Ciancutti & Steding, 2001). In short, we can say that trust is earned by consistency.

Once you lose the trust of colleagues and associates, it's very hard to regain. When sound character is the guide for effective leadership, they are consistent in their belief that is mirrored by their conduct. When honorable character is demonstrated in public, it is tested in secret when your choice or decision is made in the absence of those that know and trust you.

When consumers trust the ethical imperative out-put or product of the factory that ensures that work is done as effectively and efficiently as possible, the end results will be the production of high-quality yields from the organization. To earn trust, an effective leader has to be authentic. Authentic factories that use the raw materials, such as steel, peanuts, or a five-year-old child for their input will produce as output cars, peanut butter, and educated students that will impact the world.

John Maxwell states, "For a leader to have the authority to lead, he needs more than the title on his door. He has to have the trust of those who are following him" (Maxwell, Developing the Leader within You, 1993).

Authorities and Partisans are described by Gamson as the relationship between two antagonists that are often central to the politics of organizations and the society in which we live (Gamson, 1968). Authorities are the leaders or decision makers while partisans are usually the subordinates.

Bolan & Deal notes that, "In a family, parents function as authorities and children as partisans. Parents initiate social control and children are the recipients of parental decisions" p. 195 (Bolman & Deal, 2013).

The children trust the parent to make the right decisions for their safety and empowerment. If partisans trust authority and see it as legitimate, they will accept and support it in the event of an attack (Gamson, 1968) (Baldridge, 1971).

A child that trusts in his or her parent as the authoritative figure will defend their parent as the best parent in the world. John Maxwell states that, "Effective leadership … is not based on being clever; it is primarily on being consistent. To trust a leader, it is not necessary to agree with him or her. Trust is the conviction that the leader means what they say. A leader's action and professed beliefs must be congruent" p. 44. (Maxwell, The 21 Irrefutable Laws of Leadership. Follow Them and People Will Follow You, 1998).

Effective leaders have followers who believe that what they do is right. Followers trust the leaders to make decisions that improve human development and that of the organization. The character of an effective leader should reflect self-discipline, inner trust, and the relentless honesty in all aspects of their lives. When leaders fail to follow the principle of practicing what they preach, eventually they will lose their credibility as an effective leader. Better employee outcomes will emerge from concerted efforts to build organizations cultures on trust.

Trusting in what you believe

Noah had to choose whether to trust God and take action to prepare for the flood or trust his senses and the viewpoints of people around him. Noah's faith in God led him to build an ark that made no sense to those around him. Noah acted on his vision and it saved the life of his family when the rain came and water covered the earth.

The Wright brothers acted on their dreams of making man fly like a bird, although it made no sense to those around them. Today, the airline industry is a multi-billion dollar venture and one of the fastest growing industries, both private and commercially, that takes travelers and commodities from one end of the world to the other.

Chapter 8

Effective leadership in your area of functioning

Dr. Myles Munroe states that, "You become a leader when you discover who you are and your purpose. Take a look at an automobile engine. If you lift the hood, there are thousands of components that make up the engine and each one is different from the other" (Munroe, The Power of Character in Leadership. How Values, Morals, Ethics, and Principles Affect Leadership, 2014).

The battery is different from the spark plugs, the spark plug is different from the fuel injection system. The alternator is not a piston, a piston is not a valve, the transmission is not the brake, and the steering wheel is not the computer.

All the parts are different. However, the battery is a leader in the battery department. The battery stores power and releases it when the terminals demand it because his leadership responsibility is to produce the power to the automobile. The terminals on the battery are positive and the other negative have their purpose to transfer power when it is needed. Every component in the engine is a leader in the function for which it was made. Although the battery provides the source of power, each component where power is transferred is able to dominate its area of influences because each component can discover their purpose and how the role of each part affects the effectiveness of the automobile. The sum of the parts is greater than each individual part.

Effective leaders bring out the leadership qualities in those they lead. Imagine that the automobile has the petrol and oil and all the other components and there is no battery?

The automobile would not be able to perform the purpose for which it was made.

One of the greatest assets to effective leadership is the ability to effectively communicate with the people in the schools, organizations, and religious institutions. Effective leaders are not afraid to ensure that those they lead become independent thinkers. The confidence of the effective leader does not let him/her feel insecure when those they lead become leaders. Leadership is the ability to help others discover their own ability and take responsibility for their ability. He/she releases responsibility to each individual to lead in the area of their purpose. The battery does not dominate the other parts by suppression or oppression but realized that when all the parts are connected as a team, then the automobile can be effective. Effective leaders produce leaders.

Original Leadership Philosophy
1. Trapped in every follower is a hidden leader
2. Every human was created to lead
3. Leadership potential resides in every individual
4. The purpose for true leadership is the production of leaders (Munroe, The Power of Character in Leadership. How Values, Morals, Ethics, and Principles Affect Leadership, 2014)

Effective leaders are confident in who they are and they are not afraid to mentor and pass on important knowledge to others. Mentoring and imparting best practices will increase the effectiveness in what employees have learned and keep learning from their peers.

By empowering other people to become great, effective leaders inspire the people around them and are engendered by a sense of purpose. By discovering who you are, you pursue your purpose.

Discovering your gift

We can release the gifts within us to become effective leaders when we harness, define, and pursue the key to unlocking our vision. Education, in itself, does not always guarantee anything; it is your gift that is the key to your success (Munroe, The Principles and Power of Vision. Keys to achieving Personal and Corporate Destiny, 2003).

Success will naturally come when both your intellect and instincts are aligned (Jakes, Instinct. The Power to Unleash Your Inborn Drive, 2014).

Effective leaders are individuals who discover their gifts and develop it to the point where the world is willing to pay for your creativity.

"The 1980's were a golden era for the National Basketball Association. The on-court rivalry of Boston's Celtics Bird and Magic Johnson of the Los Angeles Lakers sparked interest in casual fans. The up tempo, high-scoring spectacles created excitement in the sporting world. Jordan was a perfect fit for the league's up-and-coming fast-breaking style… Jordan enjoyed one of the top scoring seasons of all times in 1986-87. He finished with 3,041 points. As of 2013, only Jordan and Hall of Famer, Wilt Chamberlin, had eclipsed the 3,000-point milestone in a single season" p. 39 (Hawkins, 2011).

As a child, Michael Jordan and his siblings were competitively playing basketball or football. His dad made wooden back boards and rims in their backyard where Michael learned to hone his skills as a natural athlete playing baseball, football, and eventually received a certificate of achievements for both sports in middle school. In summer months, Michael would spend most of his time practicing the game of basketball. In college, Michael spent many hours practicing his craft before school, after school, and sometimes during the school period. Michael's desire to work to improve all aspects of his game had discovered his gift that made him stand out on the court instead of just blending in as another player on his team. .

The fruits of your labor brings satisfaction beyond measure with hard work, dedication, and the internal satisfaction that fuel your desire to achieve even larger dreams (Jakes, Instinct. The Power to Unleash Your Inborn Drive, 2014).

CHAPTER 9

Collaboration and Effective Leadership

When employees are allowed to talk with each other and contribute meaningfully to solving problems and making decisions, best solutions can be achieved that will enhance the productivity of the given institution.

There is growing recognition that collaboration is an essential condition for improving employee output. Collaboration creates trust and buy-in and focuses employees on a common, achievable goal. The pursuit of collaboration entails upending top-down hierarchies that have characterized U. S. schools, houses of worship, and organizations for many decades.

Collaboratively sharing of ideas about research based best practices make employees effective at their jobs.

Building a Collaborative Culture

Effective leaders engage in activities to ensure that their organization contains a collaborative culture where individuals are empowered and the vision and decisions are shared (Dufour, Dufour, & Eake, 2008). In a collaborative culture, employees and leaders support each other by displaying collegiality, trust, openness, and professionalism. This enables effective leaders to engage in change and improvement that is essential to the success of the organization.

Collaborating Despite our Differences

On the night of November 4th, 2008, Barack Hussein Obama addressed the nation as their first African-American to be elected president of the United States. His presidency led to other unprecedented firsts. President Barack Obama had his first major introduction to the nation on July 27th, 2004 as the keynote speaker at the second day of the Democratic National Convention. The major highlight of his speech was when he said:

"Tonight, there is not a liberal and conservative America; there is the United States of America. There is not a black America and a white America and a Latino America, and an Asian America, there's the United States of America" p. 35 (Krut, 2009).

In his speech, he evoked the theme from Dr. Martin Luther King Jr. and President Abraham Lincoln.

"We hold these truths to be self-evident, that all men are created equal. That they are endowed by their creator with certain inalienable rights. That among these are life, liberty, and the pursuit of happiness" p. 35 (Krut, 2009).

Obama went on to win the nomination for the Democratic Party four years later and eventually the presidency in November 2008.

How did he do it? As candidate, Barak Hussain Obama campaigned throughout the country, he invoked the phrase, "Yes, we can," and constantly reminded the nation that there was so much more the country could accomplish when individual work collaboratively, regardless of our differences in race, political, and religious belief and family ties.

Just about any politician can make a nation feel good by offering promising benefits that they know they may never be able to provide. But leaders who leave a legacy take a different approach because they look at how they can lead change for a better future. As an effective leader, the presidential candidate, Obama, focused on the young people all across the country and was able to mobilize them through the use of social media unlike previous presidents that relied heavily on television advertisements.

Using collaboration for changes and improvement

In the educational system, an effective Superintendent will provide training to district principals to build professional capacity through collaboration by establishing professional learning communities to promote shared inquiry among teachers. The hallmark of a collaborative school culture is teachers working together to improve student learning, which is the output from the training to district principals (Green, 2013).

The same principle applies when an effective leader of an organization establishes professional capacity through collaboration with the different level of workers in the company. When employees work together with a sense of personal responsibility for production of the desired product, a synergy develops as they support one another's journey to increase productivity and the achievement of the organizations goals.

CHAPTER 10

Perseverance and Leadership

Effective leaders adjust to changes around them. In the fable of two mice that fell in a bucket of cream, the first mouse gave up and died, the second mouse struggled and struggled until he churned the cream into butter and he walked out. Effective leaders use a problem as a means of turning the problem into a learning experiences that leads to success. Dr. Myles Munroe said in a presentation that you become valuable based on the problem you solve.

Effective leadership demands perseverance

T. D. Jakes destiny states that, "It takes courage to produce what God is drawing out of you" (Jakes, Destiny. Step into Your Purpose. , 2015).

However, to be an effective leader, it takes both courage and perseverance to fulfil your purpose on earth. You will have to go above and beyond wanting to be just a leader and face the many unplanned challenges along the way. It will take perseverance to believe in yourself that you will be successful, even when doors are closing in your face. You may ask, "Why bother to go the extra mile if no doors are open?" The bible reassures us in Matthew 7:7-8, "Seek, and he shall find; knock, and it shall be opened unto you; ask, and it shall be given you" (Thompson, F. C. (2002). King James Version. The Thompson Chain-Reference Bibles. 5th Edition, 2002).

Your success as an effective leader will depend on the perseverance to start with the end in mind. Effective leaders follow their dreams or vision to accomplish their purpose in life. What will matter most is the positive relationship that effective leaders develop with employees, associates, and followers.

Perseverance means doing the right thing, even when you are criticized by people you thought were confidants. Continue working on your plans, monitoring the activities in your organization, mentoring new employees and followers. Through perseverance, you must manage trust by demonstrating that you are reliable and consistent in words and deeds. Perseverance will embolden you to learn from mistakes and focus on your success. It empowers you to use past failures as learning experience, so you can get up from the ground, shake off the dust of disappointment, and pursue your purpose.

Empowering your-self through Perseverance

Madam Walker once stated:

"I am a woman who came from the cotton field of the south. I was promoted from there to the washtub. Then I was promoted to the cook kitchen, and then from there, I promoted myself into the business of manufacturing hair goods and preparation" (Stille, 2007).

Madam Walker was an effective leader that never stopped working to improve her products and empower her employees. Her perseverance eventually made her the first African-American female millionaire. In the audience of business men at the National Negro Business League Executive committee, Walker made one of her most famous speech with the quote above.

Madam C. J. Walker recognized that hard work was required to gain influence in her organization and to earn the right to become the first African-American female millionaire. Madam Walker's motto was "perseverance."

As an American entrepreneur to an audience of approximately 200 women in 1917, she said,

"It [perseverance] gave us the telegraph, telephone, and wireless. It gave to the world an Abraham Lincoln and to a race freedom" p. 9 (Stille, 2007).

Believers often quote the Hebrews chapter in the New Testament that states, "Faith is the substance of things hope for, the evidence of things not seen."

Effective leaders are willing to take the risk, although they may not know how successful will be the outcome. If the outcome is successful for believers in faith, they will say it is the evidence that could not be seen. For non-believers, they will say it is my luck because I invested and took the chances that I did at the right time. For effective leaders, when the outcome is negative, they use the negative results as a learning opportunity to make the necessary changes that will lead to success in business, organizations, or place of worship.

CHAPTER 11

Crisis Response Plan

Effective leaders establish command and control structures that identifies the individuals who are charged with directing the response to a crisis before it occurs. This maximizes the effectiveness of the system to ensure that responsibilities of each individual in the command and control structures are clearly defined in advance for a variety of crisis situations.

Effective leaders are prepared to confront different crisis, analyze them, and know how to administer the most efficient solution. This can only be achieved when empathetic leaders listen attentively with an open mind to the individual or groups and ask relevant questions that will help them truly understand and gain information about the problem. Effective leaders feedback is effective when it is clearly understood and acted upon and staff members feel that their opinions are important as it relates to the crisis.

Laws

The primary role of the laws is to carry out the legal responsibility to protect the right of every citizen. Effective leaders use an inclusive process when developing and updating the school or organization's vision through compliance with State and Federal policies mandating the involvement of employees, families, and stakeholders in educational or industrial planning.

The laws play a role in protecting employees, students, worshipers, and the organization. Laws ensure that established policies and requirements are carried out and ensures that the proper training and certification standards are upheld. Effective leaders use laws to carryout regulations that govern the operation of the various institutions in conformation with State and Federal legislations.

Organization safety and security

"On February 14th, 2018, 17 students and staff at Marjory Stoneman Douglas High School in Parkland, Florida were fatally shot and 17 others were wounded in a school shooting (Sanchez, 2018). If the school superintendent could predict that a shooting would take place that day, he would be more prepared and that would reduce the amount of fatality.

Every employee, student, or worshiper has the right to come to the building for business, place of worship, or school and feel that their safety and security will not be compromised. An effective leader of the organization makes it their responsibility to ensure that every employee or student is safe in the environment where they work, worship, or study. They encourage employees and students to maintain and create a positive and safe environment.

Effective leaders have in place established policies with regards to violence and establishes the consequences of violent behavior. They implement organizational violence prevention programs to help employees address conflicts and give instructions on where to seek help ahead of conflicts. Effective leaders constantly use updated research and resources to help in violence prevention training programs. An effective leader must always stay informed with most recent research on violence prevention because it is more beneficial than having to deal with criminal enforcement.

Conflict management

"Conflict management is the process of addressing staff/student in a non-threatening and positive manner to resolve and minimize disagreements that result from perceived or real differences" p. 207 (Green, 2013).

Conflict is a major occurrence in today's institutions, and effective leaders are discovering that managing it can be a challenging process if a collaborative approach is not used to solve problems that may occur with and within the organization. As organizations increase in diversity, effective leaders have to be knowledgeable of the challenges that may give rise to conflict. Effective leaders must be knowledgeable in how to put in place established rules and guideline to reduce the incidence of conflict and minimizing its disruptive effect before the conflict occurs.

Effective leaders that state their true feelings to a conflict creates a more secure environment. Therefore, effective leaders need to invest time and resources with both parties to achieve the best solution to the conflict to ensure that a positive climate or environment is maintained with/in the organization.

Dealing with conflict

Effective leaders use strong interpersonal skills when dealing with conflict.

"Leaders use the cooperative and confirming approaches to conflict that enable individuals to feel recognized and have a sense of security and value in resolving conflict" p. 6 (SLLA Secrets, 2014).

The stakeholder in the conflict point of view and concerns are heard and empathy is given to the groups feelings. Effective leaders attempt to find a compromise or consensus that lead to an actual solution, taking into consideration individual's personal needs, the type of conflict, and its impact on the organization.

Consensus Building

"Consensus building allows everyone to have an opportunity to have their voices heard and opinions respected even if one party's viewpoint is preferred over the others" p.3 (SLLA Secrets, 2014).

Effective leaders always keep abreast with the latest research of products or programs that can produce concrete research-based results. The results can in turn lead to the assessment of the organization's current position. Assessment data can then be disaggregated or broken down and used to set priorities to ensure improvement in areas of the organization that need to meet the required standards.

CHAPTER 12

Embracing Diversity

"Diversity includes differences in age, gender, sexual orientation, political beliefs, socioeconomic status, religion, physical and mental ability, language, and ethnicity" (Hawkins, 2011). Should effective leaders be concerned about diversity? If you say yes, then we need to be informed about diversity.

One of the most important value of diversity is the advantage of having people with a variety of viewpoints on different state of affairs because it will be valuable in making decisions and solving problems that occurs within the various institutions.

Effective leaders respond positively to diversity and are proactive to the needs of their employees, students, and congregants. They know that when leaders act proactively to diversity, it enables the organization, educational institutions, and places of worship to improve employees' productivity and enhances student's ability in reaching maximum learning potential.

Why should effective leaders embrace diversity?

Embracing diversity incorporates knowing organization, educational institutions, and houses of worship as interactive and cultural systems that demands cultural capability for effective leadership. Instituting an organizational culture and environment that shows appreciation for diversity brings about a caring community.

Diversity in organizations

Effective leaders establish diversity policies as the norm in all organizations. The leaders, managers, and employee population are diverse, whether an organization is located in the United States or internationally or whether it consists predominantly of one race or ethnic group or a variety of cultural groups. Some organizations will have greater diversity than others.

Effective leaders ensure that their organizations acknowledge and act on diversity in their population by developing programs involving employees, families, and communities. These partnerships assist organizations in understanding families, their cultures, and background of employees. The partnership creates a two way communication channel, so that employees can easily communicate with administrators, counselors, and diverse families.

Creating an environment that fosters diversity

Effective leaders are active in establishing diversity policies, assessing the organizations environment, and communicating the desired diversity needs to the stakeholders in a manner that produce positive outcomes that are desired for all employees. The personal values of effective leaders must be balanced, diverse, and one that reflects a positive culture within the organization.

On April 12th, 2018, two African-American men were arrested in a Philadelphia Starbucks coffee store. One of the young men asked to use the bathroom. His request was denied. They were instructed to leave, although Starbucks is a place where people meet for business or come in to take advantage of the free Wi-Fi. Within two minutes, the two African-American young men were arrested by the police.

The young men said that they were waiting for a friend, but they decided to come to the store early before the meeting. They were released without charges after being arrested for eight hours. The video of the arrest went viral, and many customers from all ethnic groups started to boycott Starbucks nationally and internationally.

The boycott prompted the CEO of Starbucks to issue an apology and called for revision of the company's policies. He said that nobody should be asked to leave Starbucks and closed the 8,000 stores on May 29th, 2018 for racial bias education for approximately 175,000 U.S. employees.

Effective leaders are aware that they play a vital role in influencing, understanding, and promoting equity and diversity in their organizations through communications and professional development of staff, employees, and students. Effective leaders routinely evaluate professional development plans that are implemented to ensure that it clearly addresses equity and diversity that supports growth, democratic values, and equity practices for diverse employees, staff, students, and congregants.

Cultural differences

"Culturally responsive employees are at the heart and soul of culturally responsive institutions, but the organization as a community also has a vital role to play in addressing diversity" (Glickman, Gordon, & Ross-Gordon, 2010).

Research has shown that not all children or people from low socioeconomic backgrounds lack appropriate knowledge and skills needed to be an exceptional student or highly effective employee. Effective leaders focus on building bridges between cultures with the goal of the human relations approach that is to help all groups of people develop positive attitudes towards people of different racial, cultural, and gender identity.

Culturally Sensitive Organizations

It is the responsibility of effective leaders to create an organizational environment that is sensitive to diverse cultures. These environments must be culturally sensitive in order to successfully respond to diversity of employees and build positive relationships between the organization and diverse communities.

Prejudice is a negative outlook or belief towards a group of people that may be based on their culture, language, ethnicity, or sexual identity. Usually stereotypes are inaccurate beliefs about a group that results in prejudice leading to discrimination. The role of effective leaders is to help employees and followers see why they hold these prejudices that will lead to discrimination because of beliefs and actions that are not based on facts.

Equity

"Achieving equity requires a significant allocation of human and material resources- to ensure that all members in the organization regardless of their personal characteristics, backgrounds or physical challenges-achieve their highest potential in making the organization successful" (NCTM , 2000).

People become better communicators when there is positive interaction across racial groups. The result is an increase in racial tolerance and equity.

Equity requires high expectation for all employees, stakeholders, and students regardless of their personal characteristics, background, or physical challenges. Effective leaders have an obligation to ensure that all employees participate in strong instructional and professional development programs that support productivity of the organization. Equity requires resources and support for all employees that result in the empowerment that is key to multicultural education.

Multicultural education challenges and rejects racism and other forms of discrimination in diverse organizations. Effective leaders use multicultural education to permeate policies and instructional strategies to develop knowledge and skills that enable their employees to be critical thinkers. Culturally responsive effective leaders learn from employees, and employees share knowledge about themselves, families, and communities. Intercultural sensitivity creates organizations that integrate cultural knowledge through all its operations. Knowledge is essential for tolerance and support. Effective leadership requires that leaders promote awareness of diversity in their organizations.

Effective leaders who model and promote respect of others, kindness, and consideration of people and staff, honesty and fairness, and a constant concern for the needs of all employees set a positive example that others will want to follow.

CHAPTER 13

Legacy and effective leadership

Bishop T. D. Jakes, in his book *Soar,* states that, "You will also need faith if you want to leave a legacy that will enrich future generations" (Jakes, Soar! Build Your Vision from the Ground Up, 2017).

The American Society of Civil Engineers has called the Panama Canal one of the seven wonders of the modern world and legacy in America's engineering excellence.

The Panama Canal or in Spanish Canal de Panama is a waterway that is 48 miles long that connects the Atlantic Ocean with the Pacific Ocean.

President Theodore Roosevelt's legacy of effective leadership is that he oversaw the realization of a long-term United States goal that enabled American and British leaders and entrepreneurs to ship goods quickly and cheaply between the Atlantic and Pacific coasts.

France started work on the canal in 1881 but could not complete the project due to failed engineering technology and high worker mortality rates from Malaria, Yellow Fever, and other tropical disease. The setback for the French inspired the American interest in the completion of the canal (Panama Canal Authority, 2007).

President Roosevelt rallied the U. S. Senate who voted in favor of building the canal through Panama and supported the Panamanian independence from Columbia by dispatching U. S. warships to Panama City. The United States took over the project to build the Panama Canal in 1904 and completed the canal on August 15th, 1914. The Panama Canal symbolized U. S. technological prowess and economic power that is recognized as a major foreign policy achievement a legacy that will enrich future generations.

Choosing the legacy you want

John Maxwell reminds us that if we desire to make an impact as a leader on a future generation, he suggests that we become highly intentional about our legacy. Leaders have to choose the legacy they want (Maxwell, The 21 Irrefutable Laws of Leadership. Follow Them and People Will Follow You, 1998).

In 1993, President Clinton's healthcare plan goal was to provide universal healthcare for all Americans. The Clinton health plan required each U. S. citizen and permanent resident alien to become enrolled in a qualified health plan on his or her own or through programs mandated to be offered by businesses with more than 5,000 fulltime employees. Subsides were to be provided to the poor who could not afford coverage.

In a major healthcare speech to a joint session of Congress on September 22nd, 1993, President Clinton stated that:

"Millions of Americans are just a pink slip away from losing their health insurance and one serious illness away from losing all their savings. Millions more are locked into jobs because they or someone in their family have once been sick with what is called the preexisting condition. On any given day, over 37 million Americans – most working people and their little children – have no health insurance."

William Kristol and his policy group, Project for the Republican Future, was widely credited with orchestrating the Clinton health plan defeat. From the early 1990's to the late 2000's, millions of American citizens lost their houses and life savings because of preexisting health conditions. The cost of healthcare was high. Many people that could have been cured of illnesses if they saw a doctor early waited until they were very ill and checked themselves into hospitals, and by then, their chances of recovery were slim.

The Patient Protection and Affordable Care Act (A.C.A), or nationally called Obamacare, was signed into law by President Barak Obama on March 23rd, 2010, approximately 18 years after the introduction of the Clinton healthcare plan.

The ACA's major provisions came into force in 2014. An estimated 20 – 24 more million Americans had health insurance in 2016. The increased coverage was due to an expansion of Medicaid eligibility and to a major change to individual insurance markets. Insurers in the markets were made to accept all applicants and charge the same rates, regardless of preexisting conditions, age, or gender of the individual. To help households at the Federal Poverty Line, the law provided insurers premium subsidies.

President Barack Obama created a legacy by putting into law the healthcare of the U. S. citizens, a legacy that will carry on even after his presidency. The Affordable Care Act has faced challenges and opposition from the Republicans. In 2017-2018, a unified Republican government (President, Senate, and House of Representatives) tried to pass several different partial repeals of the ACA.

However, the law gained plurality support by 2017-2018, although the law spent several years opposed by a slim plurality of polled Americans. President Obama's effective Leadership in the stewardship of the Patient Protection and Affordable Care Act will be judged by how well the American citizens benefitted from their health insurance and the positive impact it has had on their lives long after his tenure as president of the United States.

"We're here to put a dent in the universe, otherwise, why else even be here?"

Creating opportunities for future generations is working towards creating your legacy. "Steve Jobs knew what he wanted his legacy to be before he put any product on the market. He wanted to make technology more 'humanistic'" The Steve Jobs legacy has impacted the world. After his death, each year, new Apple products are introduced to the world that is based on the visionary innovations of Steve Jobs.

Michael Essany asserts that, "50 years from now, we will be reflecting on the life and legacy of another tech visionary who shaped the future of his or her time. At the moment, we don't know who that person is or what that person will accomplish for humanity" p. 622 (Essany, 2012).

North America Free Trade Agreement

The North American Free Trade agreement came into existence during a time when President Bill Clinton saw the need to boost the unstable U.S. economy during his first term as president. The agreement between the United States, Mexico, and Canada removes the tariff on trade between these countries, which led to the beginning of the upward movement in the U.S. economy (Kent, 1994).

There were pros and cons to the trade agreements. By removing many tariffs in the agreement between Mexico, Canada, and the Unites States, the United States paid much lower prices for imported goods. Consumers benefited from the lower cost in essential products that were imported and consumers were encouraged to spend more that resulted in the positive stimulation of the economy.

However, some domestic manufactory industries suffer because the imported products cost less than the product that was made in the United States. President Clinton chose to risk the trade-off between companies and consumers.

On the other hand, some domestic industries benefited from the NAFTA because they found new markets for the exportation of their tariff-free products. Those American industries grew and hired more workers and the U.S. economy grew as it moved out of the depression and job decline over the years prior to President Clinton's term in office.

CHAPTER 14

Conclusion

If all leaders knew what the needs are for their organizations, schools/universities, place of worship employees, students and congregants, before making essential program change, they would be leaders that know how to collect data and disaggregated the information and set priorities to ensure improvement in their organizations. The leader would then become change agents that use assessment plans that provides important information about the strengths and weaknesses in current organizational operations.

The leader would then get the necessary resources that is needed for the implementation of change and put in place a mechanism for formative evaluation to assess the effectiveness of their decisions. The future summative assessment can be used as the criterion of leverage to help effective leaders identify best practices and standards that are applicable to the efficient running of the organization.

Effective leaders will mentor or provide training for staff that is based on their needs. Effective staff development will improve knowledge and specific skills.

Personal characteristics of leaders classified under the heading of personality, achievement, and status studies were conducted by Stogdill in 1948 and Green in 2013 to determine whether characteristics and traits could be used to separate successful leaders from unsuccessful leaders (Stogdill, 1948) (Green, 2013). Stogdill noted that whereas some traits were identified as being consistent with effective leadership, the traits identified often were related to situational variables (Stogdill, 1948). However, Gibbs, in 1954, and Green, in 2013, concluded that a single trait could not be used to differentiate leaders from non-leaders (Gibbs, 1954) (Green, 2013).

Notwithstanding, in research done by Collins in 2001, Daft in 1999, and Green in 2013, they concluded that there are some traits that tend to increase the likelihood of leader success and those traits are consistently found in effective leaders (Collins, Good to great: Why some companies make the leap and others don't, 2001) (Daft, 1999) (Green, 2013).

Building a Supportive Environment

Effective leaders create a supportive environment in their organizations, educational institutions, and places of worship where everyone's role is important. Administrators, employees, teachers, ancillary staff, worshippers, and students are motivated to achieve the vision and ensure that their organization achieve its highest potential. The role of effective leaders is to establish coherent standards that support the improvement of the organization by consistently providing opportunities for mentorship and professional development to employees.

Meeting with the diverse members of the organization is an effective method of getting answers to potential problems and to hone best practices that, when implemented, will become one of the strongest assets in making the organization successful.

Effective leaders are always looking for ways for employees to excel and learn from experts the desired skills and knowledge needed to positively impact the growth of the organization. A successful organization requires a strong set of standards that challenge employees at every level to be fully engaged with their craft.

Effective leaders build strong partnership with the organization's extended families and the larger community-based organizations. Strong community ties develop trusting relationships between all members of the place of worship, educational institutions, and business organizations. Once trust is established, honest collaboration can occur and the productivity of the organization will increase.

Pro-Active leadership

Highly effective leaders are proactive and begin their journey with the end in mind. They take responsibility for their actions and know how to respond to what happens next. They take time to develop an understanding of themselves.

Chesley Burnett Sullenberger III (Sully), a retired American Airlines Captain, is celebrated for his January 15th, 2009 water landing of U.S. Airways Flight 1549 on the Hudson River near Manhattan, New York after his plane was disabled by a flock of Canadian geese that struck both engines of his aircraft.

All 155 people aboard Flight 1549 survived and were rescued by nearby boats. Sully as an effective leader saw the crisis with a clear understanding of the desired goal of safely landing the disabled aircraft. Sully, who was poised and calm during the crisis, was asked, "How could you have remained so poised during the entire crisis?"

He said, "One way of looking at this was that for 42 years, I've been making regular deposits in this bank of experience, education, and training. On January 15th, the balance was sufficient, so that I could make a very large withdrawal" (Rivera, 2009).

Sully's perseverance to pursue his studies and do extensive training in his field enabled him to make the decision to land the aircraft in the Hudson River. That choice made the critical difference between saving the lives of the 155 people or taking the chance to cruise back to LaGuardia airport. Sulley's decision as an effective leader will have a positive impact on him and the 155 people on board Flight 1549 for the rest of their lives.

The decisions you make as effective leaders have a price that is not necessarily a monetary cost. Most often the cost of perseverance may mean losing some friends and family members who did not approve of you spending time to get the education and training in pursuit of your vision. Knowledge is power. Getting the best information will enhance the effectiveness of your decision. Always endeavor to make your choices based on sound information before making a final decision. If the decision you made is not the right one at that time, God works in mysterious ways and can use the negative situation to measure your organizations performance and then implement changes that create new and more effective paradigms that will improve the entire organization.

Fulfilling your purpose

When you have a vision to fulfil your life purpose, you will have to assume the responsibility for the challenges and setbacks as you make adjustments to the changes, but you have to have the perseverance to stick with your original vision. Effective leadership requires perseverance as you implement your vision, enter new adventures, growth, failure, and having to start all over again.

As you rise to new levels, you will have to increase your knowledge to maintain your growth and develop new skills. In each new environment, the skills and past experience will enable you to do self-assessment and renewal of personal qualities that are critical to developing and maintaining an effective organization. You may have reached your highest level of effective leadership, but you still have room to grow in your relationships. Get to understand your spouse, your children, your parents, and extended family in more intimate ways. Remember, they were the ones who supported you during the entire process.

Thank family for their support and encouragement, especially for their willingness to prop you up at all hours of the night and for tolerating you throughout your leadership period. Take time out to thank God for giving you the strength and the vision to become an effective leader. It is better to meet with effective leaders that have been more successful than you. Let them be your mentors. Inspiration drawn from these relationships can propel you forward in achieving the goals you create for yourself that were once dreams.

Finally, effective leaders encourage employees to participate in decision making and governance to assist families and the organization's representatives in getting information that is based on facts by collaborating with communities, businesses, agencies, cultural and civic organizations, universities, and places of worship.

END

BIBLIOGRAPHY

Baldridge, J. (1971). Power and Conflict in the University. New York: Wiley.

Bolman, L., & Deal, T. E. (2013). Reframing Organization. Artistry choice, & Leadership (5th ed.).

Carson, C. (1998). The Autobiography of Martin Luther King, Jr. Intellectual Properties Management .Inc.

Ciancutti, A., & Steding, T. (2001). Built on trust: Gaining competitive advantage in any organization. Chicago: Contemporary Books.

Collins, J. (2001). Good to great: Why some companies make the leap and others don't. New York: HarperBusiness.

Collins, J. (2005). Good to great and the social sectors. Why business thinking is not the answer. Boulder, CO: Author.

Daft, R. (1999). Leadership: Theory and Practice. Worth, TX: Harcourt College.

Dufour, R., Dufour, R., & Eake, R. (2008). Revisiting Professional Learning Community at Work. New Insight for Improving Schools.

Essany, M. (2012). Steve Jobs. Ten Lessons in Leadership.

Foremenski, T. .. (2016, February 24). The Steve Jobs way: Exploring the intersection of psychedelics and technology . Retrieved from ZDNet.

Fullan, M. (2007). The Jossey- Bass Reader on Educational Leadership (2nd ed.). The Jossey- Bass.

Fullan, M. G. (2002). The change leader. Educational Leadership, 59(8), 16-20.

Gamson, W. (1968). Power and Discontent. Florence. Florence, Ky.: Dorsey Press.

Gibbs, C. A. (1954). Leadership. (G. Lindzey, Ed.) Handbook of social psychology, 2, 877-920.

Glickman, C. A., Gordon, S. P., & Ross-Gordon, J. M. (2010). Supervision and Instructional Leadership. A Developmental Approach. (9th ed.). Pearson.

Goleman, D. (2006). The socially intelligent leader. Educational Leadership, 64(1), 76-81.

Green, R. (2013). Practicing the Art of Leadership. A Problem-Based Approach to Implementing the ISLLC Standards (4th ed.).

Guarino, S. (1974). Communication for supervisors. Columbus: Ohio State University.

Hawkins, R. J. (2011). Introduction to Educational Leadership. A custom Multi-Text for College of St. Rose and The Center for Integrated Teacher Education.

Ilian, G. (2016). Top 10 Visionaries that Changed The World. The Life and Business of Warren Buffett. 500 Life and Business Lessons.

Jakes, T. (2014). Instinct. The Power to Unleash Your Inborn Drive.

Jakes, T. (2015). Destiny. Step into Your Purpose. .

Jakes, T. (2017). Soar! Build Your Vision from the Ground Up.

Johnson, A. (1994). Automobile. History of the Auto-mobile; Automobile Industry of the World. In Encyclopedia Americana (Vol. Vol. 11, pp. 566-568).

Jung, C. (1962). Personality development ... From inside the book ... The Collected Works of C. G. Jung: Symbols of transformation.

Kanter, R. M. (1982). The middle manager as innovator. Harvard Business Review, 60(4), 95-105.

Katz, D., & Kahn, R. (1978). The social psychology of organizations (2nd ed.). New York: Wiley.

Kelly, F. C. (1994). Wilbur and Orville Wright; American Inventors. Encyclopedia Americana Vol. 29. P.556-557. In Encyclopedia Americana (Vol. Vol. 29, pp. 556-557). Kelly, F. C. (1994). Wilbur and Orville Wright; American Inventors. Encyclopedia Americana Vol. 29. P.556-557.

Kent, Z. (1994). Encyclopedia of Presidents. William Jefferson Clinton. Forty-second President of the United States.

Kramer, A. (2008). Mandela. The Rebel Who Led His Nation to Freedom. . National Geographic.

Krut, A. (2009). Barack Obama. 44th President. p. 35.

Lunenburg, F. C., & Ornstein, A. C. (1996). Educational administration: Concepts and practices (2nd ed.). Belmont CA: Wadsworth.

Mandela, N. (1990). The Struggle is my life. His Speeches and writings Brought Together with Historical Documents. New York : Pathfinder.

Marzano, R. J., Pickering, D. J., & Pollock, J. E. (2001). Classroom instruction that works. Alexandria, VA: Association of Supervision and Curriculum Development.

Marzano, R. J., Waters, T., & McNulty, B. A. (2005). School leadership that works: From research to results. Alexandria, VA: Association for Supervision and Curriculum Development.

Maxwell, J. (1993). Developing the Leader within You.

Maxwell, J. (1998). The 21 Irrefutable Laws of Leadership. Follow Them and People Will Follow You.

Munroe, M. (2003). The Principles and Power of Vision. Keys to achieving Personal and Corporate Destiny.

Munroe, M. (2009). Work Book. Discovering The Leader you were Meant to be! Becoming a Leader.

Munroe, M. (2014). The Power of Character in Leadership. How Values, Morals, Ethics, and Principles Affect Leadership.

NCTM . (2000). National Council of Teachers of Mathematics. . Principles and Standards for school Mathematics.

Nikols, F. W. (2003). Four Change management strategies. Retrieved September 10, 2007, from http://www.nickols.us@att.net.

Panama Canal Authority. (2007). A History of the Panama Canal: French and American Construction Efforts. Panama Canal Authority. Retrieved September 3, 2007

Rivera, R. (. (2009, January 16). In a Split Second, a Pilot Becomes a Hero Years in the Making . Retrieved January 17, 2009, from The New York Times: https://www.nytimes.com/ 2009/01/17/nyregion/17pilot.html?hp)

Sanchez, R. Y. (2018, March 10). "Florida Gov. Rick Scott signs gun bill" . Retrieved from CNN.

Savory, T. (2010). Abraham Lincoln. A Giant Among Presidents.

Schein, E. H. (1992). Organizational Culture and Leadership (2nd ed.). San Francisco: Jossey-Bass.

Schubert, S., & Miller, T. C. (2008, December 2008). At Siemens, Bribery Was Just a Line Item. Retrieved from New York Times: http://www.nytimes.com/2008/12/21/business/worldbusiness/21siemens.html

Schuman, M. (1999). Bill Clinton. United States Presidents.

Scott, W. (2003). Organizations: Rational, natural, and open systems (5th ed.). Upper Saddle River, NJ: Prentice Hall.

Scott, W. R., & Davis, G. F. (2007). Organizations and Organizing: Rational, Natural, and Open Systems Perspectives. Englewood Cliffs, N.J.: Prentice-Hall.

SLLA Secrets. (2014). School Leaders Licensure Assessment. Study Guide. Your Key to Exam Success.

Smith, M. E. (2002, August 25). Success rates for different types of organizational change. Retrieved from Performance Improvement, 41(1): http://www.ispi.org

Sousa, D. (2003). The Leadership Brain. How to Lead Today's Schools More Effectively.

Stille, D. (2007). Madam C. J. Walker. Entrepreneur and Millionaire. Special Lives in History that became Signature Lives.

Stogdill, R. M. (1948). Personal factors associated with leadership: A survey of the literature. Journal of Psychology, 25, 35-71.

Thompson, F. C. (2002). King James Version. The Thompson Chain-Reference Bibles. 5th Edition. (2002). King James Version. The Thompson Chain-Reference Bibles (5th ed.).

Walsh, K. (1997). Ronald Regan. Biography. . A Balliett & Fitzgerald Book.

Webster. (1995 International Edition). Webster Comprehensive Dictionary (Vol. Vol. 1 & 2.).

Wellington, E. (2018, January 4). Tarana Burke: Me Too movement can't end with a hashtag. Retrieved from Philly: Philly.com